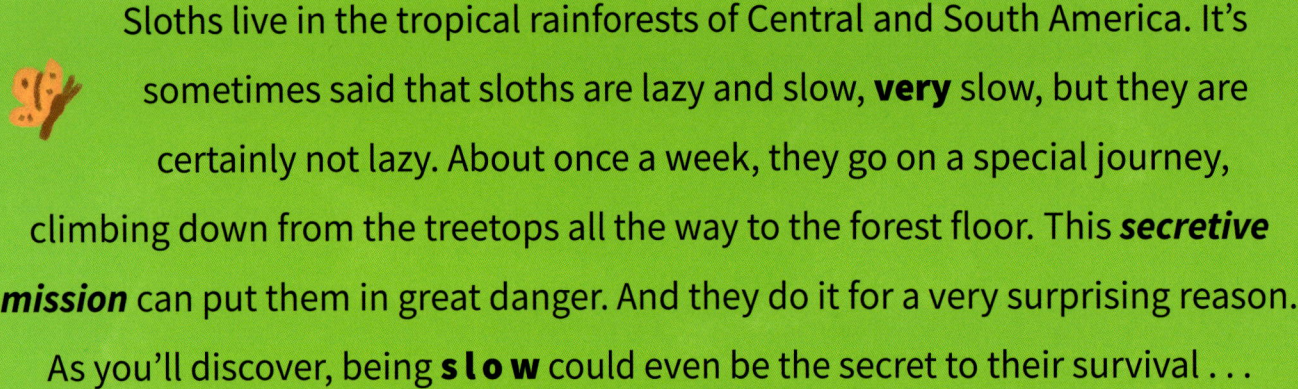

Sloths live in the tropical rainforests of Central and South America. It's sometimes said that sloths are lazy and slow, **very** slow, but they are certainly not lazy. About once a week, they go on a special journey, climbing down from the treetops all the way to the forest floor. This *secretive mission* can put them in great danger. And they do it for a very surprising reason. As you'll discover, being **s l o w** could even be the secret to their survival . . .

Thanks to Dr. Becky Cliffe. For Felix—who loves sloths.
To Cora, who wrote this first—never stop telling stories. With love always.
JA x

To my dad, who taught me the love for nature.
MM

First US edition 2025
First published by Walker Books Ltd. (UK) 2025

Library of Congress Catalog Card Number pending
ISBN 978-1-5362-3962-1

25 26 27 28 29 30 CCP 10 9 8 7 6 5 4 3 2 1

Printed in Shenzhen, Guangdong, China

This book was typeset in Source Sans Pro.
The illustrations were done in mixed media.

Candlewick Press
99 Dover Street
Somerville, Massachusetts 02144

www.candlewick.com

EU Authorized Representative: HackettFlynn Ltd.,
36 Cloch Choirneal, Balrothery, Co. Dublin, K32 C942, Ireland.
EU@walkerpublishinggroup.com

CANDLEWICK PRESS

READY, STEADY, SLOTH!

Justin Anderson

illustrated by
Manu Montoya

High up in the forest canopy,
hidden among the leaves,
there is a sloth.
She doesn't move much,
and everything she does,
she does very **s l o w l y**.

2

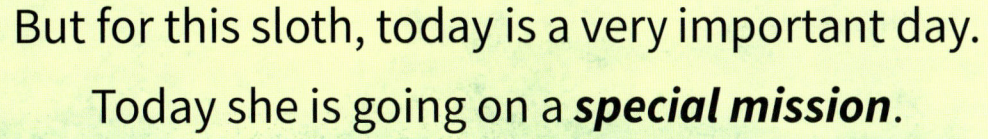

But for this sloth, today is a very important day.
Today she is going on a **special mission**.

Despite their reputation
for laziness, sloths sleep
for only eight to ten hours a
day. Cheetahs—the fastest land
animals on the planet—can sleep
for twelve hours a day.

Our sloth won't be alone on her journey.
Snuggled tightly to her is a small baby.

A female three-fingered sloth gives birth hanging upside down.
She raises one baby at a time without any help.

4

His mom is his whole world,
and she carries him all the time.
She is like a warm, furry hammock,
dangling in the treetops.

As soon as they are born, baby sloths crawl up onto their mother's chest and stay there for the next six months.

Our sloth and her baby are **hungry**.

So, before they go anywhere, she uses her **l o n g   a r m s** to reach out to the tips of the branches and grab the most tender new leaves.

Three-fingered sloths mostly just eat leaves. To help digest all this tough vegetation, they have a large four-chambered stomach filled with helpful gut bacteria (humans have only one chamber).

As Mom chews,
she lets her baby taste
the leaves in her mouth.
This is how she teaches
him which ones are
good to eat.

It might take you two to five days
to digest a whole meal, but it
can take a sloth thirty days to
digest a single leaf.

With their bellies now full,
there is no time to lose . . .

Ready,
steady,
GO!

Oh dear . . .

Our sloth hasn't
moved at all.

But sloths are never in a hurry, and very slowly, she begins to climb down the tree.

With her baby on board, her secret mission begins!

Sloths are the slowest-moving of all mammals. They have a top speed of 1½ miles (2.4 kilometers) per hour. The fastest a human can run is about 27 miles (44 kilometers) per hour. Cheetahs can reach speeds of about 70 miles (110 kilometers) per hour.

Our sloth uses her **long claws** as hooks to cling on tightly.

Sloths' claws are in fact the bones of their fingertips. They can lock in place, meaning sloths can spend up to 90 percent of their time hanging upside down.

It's a
long
way
down.
But it's a journey she has
taken many times before.
Her baby peeps out,
enjoying the ride.

On average, a sloth will fall
out of its tree once a week. They
can fall over 100 feet (30 meters)
without injury because all sloths are
designed to survive the impact. Some types
of sloths (known as two-fingered sloths)
have forty-six ribs, which help cushion the
fall (humans have only twenty-four).
Three-fingered sloths have only
twenty-eight ribs but are still
designed to survive a fall.

It's very hard to spot our sloth in the trees,
even when she is moving.

Tiny life-forms grow on her hairs,
making her fur a dirty green color that
helps her blend in with the forest.

Tiny plantlike life-forms called algae make sloths the only green-colored mammals. Sloths' fur has tiny microscopic cracks, which provide a home for eighty different kinds of algae and tiny fungi.

Her body is also crawling with small brown moths. She is a bit like a slow-moving compost heap!

Scientists have discovered at least five species (types) of moth that live only on sloths. If you count all the plants, insects, and bacteria carried by one sloth, you'll find it is home to about a million living things.

Finally, at the bottom of the tree,
it's time for our sloth to complete her mission.
But what is she here to do?

14

Holding
the tree trunk,
she **shuffles** her
rear end . . .

she **waggles**
her tail to dig
a small hole,
and then . . .

15

she takes a big poop!

Sloths only poop about once a week! But they poop a lot—up to a third of their entire body weight in one go. What a relief! Scientists call the shuffle—when sloths wag their tails to dig a hole—a "poop dance."

After Mom goes, it's her baby's turn. The sloths then bury their poop with leaves.

Scientists think the poop could be a smelly signal to other sloths and might be a way for males to find female sloths. If sloths just pooped up in their trees, the poop would land all over the place and be harder for other sloths to find.

But there is **_danger_**
here on the ground.
A jaguar is coming
through the forest . . .

Jaguars are the largest big cat in the Americas. They have powerful jaws that can break through a turtle's shell. If they get the chance, they will hunt sloths too.

The sloth
and her baby
f r e e z e.

The jaguar stops.
Turning his huge head,
he looks around . . .
but he **sees nothing**.

The jaguar sniffs the air . . . but he **can't smell anything**.

He listens . . . but he **doesn't hear a thing**.

Sloths are able to stay very still, and their algae makes them smell like the forest. They also don't fart or burp—their unusual stomachs mean they can't. There's nothing to give them away to a predator!

So he disappears back into the trees.

Saved by their slowness, our sloth and
her baby can return to the treetops.
Until next week, when it's time
for **another epic mission**.

Sloths aren't so lazy after all!

Sloths are often faster climbing
back up their trees. Maybe that's
because, having taken a big poop,
they are now much lighter!

A NOTE FROM THE AUTHOR

There are seven different species of sloth: five with three claws on each forehand (called three-fingered) and two with two claws (called two-fingered). All of them live in the tropical forests of Central and South America and eat a diet of leaves and fruit.

THREE-FINGERED SLOTHS

Brown-throated sloths—These are the best known and most common of all sloths. They weigh up to 14 pounds (about 6.5 kilograms), can live for more than thirty years, and are famous for their dark eye stripes and face that looks like it's always smiling. The mother and baby from our story are brown-throated sloths.

Pale-throated sloths
These live in the forests of the northern coastline of South America. Unlike their brown-throated cousins, they have a pale patch of yellow fur on their throats.

Northern maned sloth
Reaching a length of up to 30 inches (75 centimeters), this is the largest three-fingered sloth. Found only in a small forest area along the eastern coast of Brazil, it has a dark mane of fur around its neck.

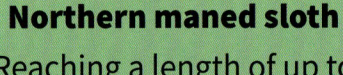

Southern maned sloth
Only discovered in 2022, this sloth is closely related to the northern maned sloth and has a head that looks a bit like a coconut.

Pygmy sloth—The rarest sloth (they are critically endangered) lives only on one small island in Panama. Weighing just 6½ pounds (3 kilograms), they are the smallest type of sloth. They are also excellent swimmers!

TWO-FINGERED SLOTHS

Hoffmann's sloth

Linnaeus's sloth

These sloths are bigger than their three-fingered cousins and move just a bit quicker. They don't have dark eye stripes, but they do have a nose that looks a little like a pig's.

FIND OUT MORE

While it's hard to be sure exactly how many sloths live hidden in the trees, we do know that they face an uncertain future. Their rainforest homes are being cut down faster than ever before, and sloths cannot outrun the destruction. To find out more about sloths, the threats to their survival, and what you can do to help, visit the Sloth Conservation Foundation website: slothconservation.org.
And to find practical, creative, and fun ways to fundraise and sponsor an area of the sloth's rainforest home, visit rainforestconcern.org.

INDEX